THE WAR MACHINE

A play by

Johnny Alspaugh

Copyright © 2016 Johnny Alspaugh

All rights reserved.

ISBN-13: 978-0692649893 (Glen Publishing)

DEDICATION

For David Israel Francis, Rest In Peace cuz.

The English language stock and amateur stage performance rights in the United States, its territories and Canada for THE WAR MACHINE are controlled exclusively by Johnny Alspaugh, johnnyalspaugh1@gmail.com, 4352 Harbinson Ave. La Mesa, CA 91942. No professional or nonprofessional performance of the Play may be given without obtaining in advance the written permission of Johnny Alspaugh and paying the requisite fee.

CAUTION: Professionals and amateurs are hereby warned that performance of THE WAR MACHINE is subject to payment of a royalty. It is fully protected under the copyright laws of the United States of America, and of all countries covered by the International Copyright Union (including the Dominion of Canada and the rest of the British Commonwealth), and of all countries covered by the Pan-American Copyright Convention, the Universal Copyright Convention, the Berne Convention, and of all countries with which the United States has reciprocal copyright relations. All rights, including without limitation professional/amateur stage rights, motion picture, recitation, lecturing, public reading, radio broadcasting, television, video or sound recording, all other forms of mechanical, electronic and digital production, transmission, and distribution, such as CD, DVD, the Internet, private and file-sharing networks, information storage and retrieval systems, photocopying, and the rights translation into foreign languages are strictly reserved. Particularly emphasis is placed upon the matter of readings, permission for which must be secured from the Author in writing.

CAST

Cole Hopkins – Late 20s. Former Army Ranger. Male.

Daria Kandt – 30s. Former Army Paratrooper. Female.

David "Dee" Koppenhaver – Early 20s. Former Marine Force Recon. Male.

Roland Longfellow – 40s. Former Army Special Forces Team Leader. Male.

Kelly Hopkins – Late 20s. Female.

Dr. Portia Ellis – 50s. Female.

Various Off-Stage Voices. Male or Female.

WHEN

Circa 2010.

WHERE

New York City…Mosul, Iraq… Landstuhl Regional Medical Center, Germany …Baghdad, Iraq

PRODUCTION

THE WAR MACHINE was produced by the author and presented at the 2016 Venus/Adonis Festival in February 2016 at the Hudson Guild Theater, New York City. It was directed by Zeke Hunter and assistant directed/choreographed by Wes Seals. The cast was as follows:

COLE HOPKINS........................Justin Wagner

DARIA KANDT......................Isabelle Van Vleet

DAVID "DEE" KOPPENHAVER....Diego Aguirre

ROLAND LONGFELLOW...............Ross Baron

KELLY HOPKINS...............................Jordan Spoon

DR. PORTIA ELLIS.....................Jennifer Suter

Prologue

Lights up. Up-Stage, Dee, Roland, Kelly, Daria and Dr. Ellis stand at attention. Down-Stage, Cole Hopkins stands in U.S. Army uniform, combat gear, holding his weapon.

Cole is an outwardly calm man with a nightmarish rage hiding just below the surface. Civilian life bores the hell out of him although he'd never admit it aloud. He is intelligent enough to understand the weight of his experiences but unable to really cope with them. He is a veteran of the campaigns in Afghanistan and Iraq. On one occasion in Iraq, he almost had his throat slit by an insurgent while he was sleeping. He still reacts violently when someone touches him in his sleep. That is, of course, when he's able to sleep: when the explosions and god-awful images retreat long enough for him to find some temporary peace. Despite everything that's happened to him, he still secretly yearns for combat; it's seeped into his blood and infected his brain. He both loves it and loathes it in equal measure. He knows that war is slowly killing him...but he has no other choice.

He speaks to the audience:

<u>COLE</u>: What experience from my service best illustrates my ability to work well with others? Well, uh, let me think...(*pause*)...Um, there are just too many stories. Okay, here we go -- this is actually a funny story. I suppose. So, in Afghanistan there are these truck called 'jingly trucks' and they're these Citroen trucks that are all painted up in these bright, obnoxious colors. They have all these tassels clinking around that makes this jingling sound. That's why they have that name. Anyway, my platoon's in this convoy of Humvees, five strong; we're about to start a patrol in the Helmand mountains and we're on this narrow road along this hill. I'm in the first Humvee and I see one of these jingly trucks coming toward us down the road. Now, the road is only wide enough for one Humvee or one jingly truck, so something's got to give. One side's a cliff and the other side's a sheer drop. We say, 'let's do this' and charge ahead. 'To hell with that guy,' we say. He'll move. My squad mates are waving him off the road like, 'get the f...get off the road.' But the jingly truck keeps coming. We're playing chicken with this guy and we're about to collide. At the last minute this guy pulls off the road and disappears down the drop. Our gunner starts yelling and he's pointing off the road. We stop and

look down and the jingly truck is rolling over and over down the embankment. Finally, it hits a snag and stops. I hop out. Everyone's like, 'what are you doing, it's his fault, don't help that guy, it's his fault.' I don't care; this guy just rolled his five-ton truck one hundred feet down a steep embankment, I'm going to see if he's okay, get a thumbs up at the very least, right? So, I hustle down the embankment and if I gotta do it alone, then I guess I'm going to do it alone, you know? The driver's alive and he's freaking out because he's stuck.

The rest of the cast moves forward to assemble the set and dress Cole for the next scene.

COLE: As the truck was going over and over, the doors got mangled and the windows were all smashed. The only way he's getting out is if we can pry the door open. I call my guys and I say, you know, 'help us out.' One guy comes down, then two, then three, finally the whole squad's there prying the driver's door open. Five minutes later, the driver's out, I shake his hand, look him over. He's okay, just a little dinged up. Found out the guy was just on his way home after selling his wares at the market. We get him some water and send him along in another jingly truck that was heading the same way he was.

Daria Kandt sits at her desk. Corner Officer With a View. New York City. 2010.

Daria is a woman of indeterminable age. She is stoic, genteel and above everything else: business.

She wears a plain pant-suit and her hair is conservatively styled. Her desk is relatively bare except for a computer, a few pens and a short stack of forms before her -- a security contract for operations in Iraq. There are no family pictures or items of sentiment to be found. On the wall above her desk hang a framed college diploma, her U.S. Army 'Honorable Discharge' certificate and a large, framed blood-stained American flag. The last piece of personal 'flair' Daria allows herself is a framed decree (which should be readable from the audience) that reads: Trustwell Security Solutions/A Partner in the United States' Global War On Terror/Proudly Defending Freedom Est. 2001. She reads a CV as the lights come up on...

Scene One.

COLE: (*pause*): So, that's it.

DARIA: (*pause*) So, I sent you the details of our contracts, pay and so forth...do you have any thoughts about which kind of contract you might be interested in?

COLE: I do. I think $98,000 towards the second contract listed with the Blue Coss/Blue Shield option would be sufficient.

DARIA: 98K with the insurance option? No. I think you should reacquaint yourself with the details of the contract because $98,000 is way more than we're willing to pay. Maximum pay-out, emphasize maximum, is $72,000.

COLE: That's guard pay!

DARIA: Well, that's what you'll be, a guard.

COLE: That's Ugandan guard pay.

DARIA: I can tell you from personal experience that a Ugandan guard does not make anything close to this.

COLE: Yeah, but...

DARIA: What was the funny part of that story?

COLE: Oh, well, I like to say that if I hadn't rallied the rest of my squad to help the driver that he'd still be down there in that ravine. Scratching away. 'Help!'

DARIA: (*snorting*) What?

COLE: Yeah. In Afghanistan, wrecks on the side of the road are so common that unless they see the accident, nobody stops to help. They're more likely to strip the thing clean before ever looking inside. The driver would still be in there if it wasn't for me.

DARIA: Uh-huh. Well, what I got from that story is a little different. I got that instead of following the rest of your team and doing what was expeditious, you chose to do what was right.

COLE: That's right. (*pause*) Something wrong?

DARIA: I'd say so. Risking yourself and the rest of your squad to help an Afghan in a wreck--

COLE: That *we* caused.

DARIA: It doesn't matter whose fault it was. What matters is your reaction to the situation. And your reaction was to put an Afghan civilian first and your squad second. Where was your squad leader during all this?

COLE: I was the squad leader.

DARIA: Mr. Hopkins, you don't seem to understand--

COLE: It was my call and everybody came home that day, including the Afghan. I stand by my performance. We did what needed to be done and I would do it again in a heartbeat if given the chance. So, with that in mind, do you mind tacking a few more zeroes on that number?

DARIA: This is not a negotiation.

COLE: It's not? You could've fooled me. You deal in contracts, correct?

DARIA: That's correct.

COLE: You assign dollar amounts to these contracts, right?

DARIA: Right again.

COLE: So, you are in a position to negotiation, whether you know it or not.

DARIA: (*pause*) Okay, lay it out for me again.

COLE: 98K for the 6 week on, 3 week off schedule with a Blue Cross/Blue Shield option, an *option*, not a guarantee.

DARIA: You do realize the kind of talent we have under contract? Just answer me this: why should we even consider your offer $98,000 when we have a Medal of Honor recipient who is willing to do essentially the same job for less?

COLE: (*pause*) Because it's not about an individual's medals; it's about the individual and what that individual has to offer. Look, I'm sure this other guy was a great soldier and an even better contractor but I'll tell you what, I'm better on all fronts. Maybe it's arrogant as hell, maybe I'm talking out of my ass but I'm willing to bet that when the time comes around to renew *my* contract, you'll be *offering me* even more money. I'll stake all $98,000 dollars on that.

DARIA: That is bold. Some might say foolish.

COLE: And some might say it's dead-on.

DARIA: (*pause*) 98K at this schedule? (*pause*) Nah, I can do 76K with the option. I can't go any higher.

COLE: You've read my service evaluations.

DARIA: I have. But there's nothing in here that would indicate that any of your experience or training or length of service is worthy of almost $100,000 of this company's money for six months of work. Let me ask you something: why do you want to be under contract with this company? Honestly.

COLE: I think this company is a crucial element to the defensive strategy of this nation. I think they are helping to keep the world safe for democracy and our allies--

DARIA: Again. Tell me, why do you want to work for this company, Trustwell Security Solutions?

COLE: (*pause*) The honest answer?

DARIA: Please.

COLE: I'm bored. On top of which, I don't know how to do anything else. I really don't. My wife got me a job as a safety instructor at some paintball place and they fired me two weeks in. Not proud of that.

DARIA: What'd they fire you for?

COLE: Participating in the paintball matches.

DARIA: Isn't that your job?

COLE: No, I was *participating* in the matches. I was participating and shooting the customers. They found out after I shot a kid in the throat.

DARIA: Ah, I see.

COLE: Look, I'm just trying to be honest. This is all I know. I was a good soldier. No, I was a great soldier. And I know that I'm asking for a lot but it would mean a lot if you could find some way to make this schedule work for the amount we talked about. Anything you can do.

DARIA: (*looking over Cole's paperwork*) It says here, Mr. Hopkins, that you have a wife.

COLE: Yeah. She's wonderful.

DARIA: Kids?

COLE: Nah, not yet. I have to get rid of my paintball guns first.

DARIA: Your wife orders?

COLE: Exactly. (*pause*) Look, I not trying to bullshit you or scam you or put in an awkward position but I have to make at least $86,000. I just can't manage anything else. I've got bills, I've got my wife's student loans, I've got cars that need to be paid off. We're looking to buy a house. I just need something to put us in the green...for once.

DARIA: $86,000? I just can't do that. I'm sorry.

COLE: What did you do before all this? This office. This title. All this?

DARIA: It doesn't matter. That's not relevant.

COLE: Fine. But somebody gave you chance. Somebody put their ass on the line for you. To get you here. Somebody believed in what you had to offer. All I'm asking you is to apply that same belief in me. I'm not capable of letting people down. That's just not in my nature.

DARIA: (*pause*) 86?

COLE: Thank you.

DARIA: That wasn't a yes. How's your Arabic?

COLE: Basic. Conversational. A little bit of Pashto too.

DARIA: Good. Realize that if we do this for you, the company is investing a lot of resources in you and your capabilities and your ability to make decisions on the fly. You need to be on point at all times and we cannot have you deviating from any of the protocols at any time. Is that understood?

COLE: Sure.

DARIA: No, is it understood?

COLE: Yes, I understand.

DARIA: Good. Okay. $86,000 with the Blue Cross/Blue Shield option. This does not leave this room. The only people who will know about this will be me, you, and the partners.

COLE: Thank you.

DARIA: I file this and then we wait for your D.o.D. background check to come back. If everything checks out, you'll be in-country within 30 days. What you need to worry about now is getting your affairs in order: your life insurance if you have it. If you don't have it, you should get it. Also, make sure your will and any legal paperwork is sorted out. I'm sure your wife is more than capable of handling any problems that arise but you don't want her to have to send a piece of paper some 8,000 miles for a signature. You'll get an email when the background check clears explaining all the itinerary and details you need. Be on the lookout for that. I think that's it. Is there anything else I can do for you today?

COLE: No, I think that's it. Just point me in the direction of the bad guys!

DARIA: Great. (*rising, extending her hand*) Mr. Hopkins, it's been an ordeal. You have an excellent day.

COLE: (*shaking her hand*) You're a miracle-worker. Thank you. I won't let you down.

DARIA: Please don't.

Light down. The cast removes the scenery in preparation for the next scene. Other cast members dress and equip Cole for the next scene:

Scene Two.

An eardrum-shattering explosion erupts from the theater's speakers. It is absolutely deafening -- anyone a little sleepy coming into this play will be wide awake at the end of this sequence. The close report of machine-gun fire can be heard. This god-awful noise continues for approximately five seconds before dying down to a tolerable (read: softer) level.

COLE: (*in blackness*) Help! HELP ME! Medic, I need a fucking medic!

Lights up on a stage littered with crumbling concrete blocks, garbage and fallen telephone wires. The light and heat are blinding.

This is Mosul, Iraq -- two months later...

(Barely) standing in the middle of this shit-show is Cole. He is now a Private Military Contractor with Trustwell Security Solutions, operating in the heart of Iraq's insurgency. He is bleeding profusely from a wound in the back of his neck caused by a piece of shrapnel. His legs are weak from shock. He is frantic. he pulls at his web gear and tries to wipe the blood from his hands. He chokes his words out--

COLE: (*re: the blood on his hands*) Oh, fuck! No, not like this! Ah, goddammit. Medic! I need a fucking medic! Please! Somebody help me!

Cole collapses.

Two other Trustwell Contractors, Dee and Roland enter with weapons ready. They hustle to help Cole. Bullets smack into the ground around them and whiz over-head. Men scream, Off-Stage. This is a chaotic mess.

Dee is an imposing, tattooed ex-Marine of mixed ethnicity. Not a naturally violent or angry man but he can turn it on when necessary. He is a professional soldier despite his incessant diarrhea of the mouth.

Roland is older than both Cole and Dee. He is worldly and compassionate but not without an edge.

DEE: (*into his radio*) Cover us! Fucking cover us!

ROLAND: (*to Cole*) Come on, man. Let's get up. Come on.

COLE: I can feel my skull. I can stick my finger in the hole and feel my fucking skull!

ROLAND: You're gonna be fine, dude. Just stand up. You can stand. Just stand up. Stand the fuck up.

DEE: Come on, man, we gotta go!

ROLAND: Fucking stand up!

DEE: Drag him.

ROLAND: God-fucking-dammit he's heavy. Help me drag him.

DEE: Let's go! (*into his radio*) Fucking cover us!

ROLAND: Hold up.

Roland removes a bandage from his medical pack and quickly applies it to the wound on Cole's head. Meanwhile--

DEE: No time for that shit, let's go!

ROLAND: Hold your fucking horses. (*to Cole*) You still with us?

Cole nods.

ROLAND: (*to Dee*) Make sure he doesn't pass out.

Roland finishes dressing Cole's wound.

ROLAND: Let's go!

Roland and Dee drag Cole off-stage.

The volume of the automatic rifle fire increases back to the previously deafening level. Again, this lasts only long enough to not completely deafen our audience. Over the transition, the sounds of Cole groaning in pain can be heard...

Blackout. Again the cast moves the set into place

and dresses Cole:

Scene Three.

2.5 days later. U.S. Army hospital - Landstuhl Regional Medical Center near Ramstein Air Base, Germany.

Lights up in the recovery ward. Cole's groaning and moaning continues until...he almost jumps out of his skin in fright, awakening from a nightmare, his head wrapped in a thick bandage...

COLE: AHHHHH! FUCK! JESUS-FUCKING-SHIT! LET ME GO! LET ME GO--!

Kelly, Cole's wife, enters and crosses to her husband. She is a small, almost insignificant woman save for her intellect and desire for "normalcy." Her life has been humane but she is not naive to the horrors of the world -- particularly the horrors of combat.

KELLY: Hey, hey, hey, it's okay. You're fine. Just breath, okay? You're fine. Just breathe.

COLE: Holy shit, holy shit, holy shit...what are you doing here?

KELLY: I had to see you, you fool. Are you okay?

COLE: Yeah...I'm just...It's good to see you.

KELLY: You had another nightmare.

COLE: Shit, yeah. Jesus Christ. (*he moves his head, winces*) Ah, man.

KELLY: You need me to get the nurse?

COLE: No, fuck it. It'll pass. I just gotta remember to keep my head still. (*beat*) God, it's good to see you. Come here.

They kiss.

COLE: (*wincing*) Ah, fuck. Careful, careful.

KELLY: I'm sorry.

COLE: It's fine. Just be careful.

KELLY: It's good to see that you're alright. When I heard...it was...I was at work and I got a phone call from Trustwell telling me what had happened.

COLE: You took time off?

KELLY: Yeah...

COLE: How long?

KELLY: Long enough. (*pause*) Are the doctors taking care of you?

COLE: Yeah. It's a little much sometimes with the exams and questions but I suppose they mean well.

KELLY: (*pause*) It's really great to see you. People have been asking about you, whether you're okay or not.

COLE: What do you say?

KELLY: I tell them that it'll take more than an I.E.D. to stop someone like you.

DEE: (*off-stage*) Lemme get in there! Oh yeah! Here we go!

Dee enters.

DEE: Let me at 'em.

Dee leaps on the Cole's bed and begins humping Cole.

DEE: (*humping away*) Oh, yeah! Y'all like that? D-Dubs is going to fuck you silly! How do you like that?

KELLY: Thank you, David...

COLE: Alright, Dee...ow, shit.

KELLY: No, seriously Dave, he's hurt.

DEE: What do you mean, he's hurt? Tis but a scratch, my lady. I stub my toe there's more blood than that.

COLE: Dee, I'm actually getting kinda hard.

DEE: (*hopping off*) Whoa! Ha! You motherfucker.

Roland enters.

DEE: Ha! A new victim!

Dee rushes over to Roland and begins humping him.

ROLAND: Off me...now.

DEE: Oh, fuck you.

Roland applies a choke-hold to Dee.

ROLAND: You just don't know when to quit, do you?

DEE: (*choking*) Fuck...tap...TAP, MOTHERFUCKER!

Roland lets him go.

DEE: Fucking ass-hat.

ROLAND: (*to Dee*) Walk away. How's it going, Cole?

COLE: I've been better.

ROLAND: No worse for the wear. Kelly: good to

see you again.

KELLY: You as well. David.

Dee lights up a cigarette.

DEE: (*to Cole*) When you coming back?

KELLY: (*to Dee*) What are doing? There's no smoking in here.

DEE: Really? This is Germany, people smoke fucking everywhere. Why not here?

KELLY: Why do you think? It's a hospital! There are sick people here. Use your head.

DEE: This is...Am I outta line here? I just want a fucking cigarette. What is this third degree shit?

ROLAND: Put the fucking cigarette out. Or go outside. Seriously.

DEE: Alright. I'm gonna be fucking irritable as hell until we leave.

ROLAND: And how would that be any different from any other time?

DEE: You know what?

ROLAND: What?

Dee puts out the cigarette in some very obnoxious manner.

<u>DEE:</u> (*to Cole*) When you coming back? When you coming back to the shit?

<u>COLE:</u> I dunno.

<u>DEE:</u> What do you mean, you dunno? They've given you a discharge date, yeah? You know what: fuck this. I'm gonna go find that doctor and get him to tell you when you can get the hell outta here.

<u>KELLY:</u> No, no, that's okay.

<u>DEE:</u> Nah, it ain't. You deserve to know. Am I wrong? Am I wrong?

<u>ROLAND:</u> No, you're not wrong, you're just a fucking crazy-person.

<u>DEE:</u> I'm crazy? I'm crazy? You're a fag.

<u>ROLAND:</u> And you're on meth.

<u>DEE:</u> Fuck you.

<u>ROLAND:</u> (*to Cole*) Stitches?

<u>COLE:</u> Yep. 33 by my last count.

<u>ROLAND:</u> 33? 33's an odd number. They never give you an odd number of stitches, it's bad luck.

KELLY: Is that true?

ROLAND: Who knows. It's just a well-known practice.

DEE: (*beat; to Roland*) God, I fucking hate you.

ROLAND: Yeah, no shit.

DEE: You just...

ROLAND: Yeah?

DEE: You know what you do?

ROLAND: No, tell me.

DEE: You sit there--

ROLAND: I'm standing, numb-nuts.

DEE: Fucking whatever! You sit there and you drop all these little bombs like that and you just, like, never explain yourself.

ROLAND: I don't have to explain myself.

DEE: Yes, you fucking do.

ROLAND: No, I don't. And it doesn't matter, you wouldn't understand it anyway -- it doesn't have to do with xBox or cocks.

DEE: You know what? Fuck you.

ROLAND: Yeah, well, what are you going to do about it?

DEE: You're lucky I don't fucking kill you, bitch!

KELLY: Hey, hey, hey, hey! What the hell are you guys doing? This is a hospital. Take it outside.

ROLAND: (*to Kelly*) I'm sorry.

DEE: Yeah, you better be.

COLE: (*to Kelly*) Baby, this is what they do. Eventually, one of them will bend the other over a desk and they'll fuck and a lot of people, myself included, will make a ton of money. Vegas odds.

DEE: Fuck you.

COLE: Yeah, fuck me, fuck you, fuck him -- what do you guys want?

ROLAND: We come bearing news.

DEE: And questions.

COLE: Oh yeah?

ROLAND: News that Trustwell has agreed to give you a fairly significant raise to help cover your 'pain and suffering' and time out of the field.

KELLY: That's great!

COLE: They could've called to tell me that. They didn't need to send you two.

DEE: Aw hell, man. We wanted to come see you. And you know me -- I'll jump on any chance to come to the land of the frau-leins. Get my swirve on, you know what I mean? Uh!

ROLAND: I can't tell you the exact dollar amount but it's gotta be pretty significant from the way they were talking about it.

COLE: (*pause*) Oh. That's good.

DEE: (*to Roland*) Ask him about the...

ROLAND: Just calm down. I'll ask him. (*to Cole*) Is it true what we've been hearing?

COLE: I don't know, what have you been hearing?

DEE: We just been hearing some shit. That's all. Shit about how you wanna break your contract, that 'this shit don't sit right with you anymore' -- that kinda shit.

COLE: What?

ROLAND: People talk, Cole. Rumors, hearsay and such. Is it true?

COLE: What's it matter?

ROLAND: Well, is it true or not?

KELLY: Is what true?

COLE: Nothing, honey.

COLE: And Dee, rumors don't equal facts. Fuck what you heard.

DEE: So you're staying?

KELLY: What's he talking about?

ROLAND: Well, before we left, Mike, you remember Mike? Dumpy-looking guy?

KELLY: Sure.

ROLAND: Well, Mike heard that Salamon, the Ugandan guard, now has Cole's Hot-Rod Magazine posters hanging up in his bunk. And I remember Cole telling me that if anything ever happened to him -- good or bad -- he left for good, for whatever reason, Salamon could have his Hot Rod posters because Salamon loves Hot Rods. How the fuck a Ugandan knows about Hot Rods is beyond me but whatever. Salamon having those posters means you're leaving for good. That's what you said.

COLE: (*pause*) No.

ROLAND: Do you mean 'no' as no, you didn't say that?

KELLY: (*pause*) Cole...

COLE: What?

DEE: So, you leaving or what?

COLE: (*pause*) I haven't decided.

KELLY: No, you can't.

DEE: I told you! (*re: Roland*) I told this motherfucker! (*to Roland*) Cough it up!

ROLAND: I ain't paying you shit.

COLE: (*to Kelly*) What do you mean, I can't?

KELLY: I just...I thought everything was going like it's supposed to.

COLE: Obviously not.

KELLY: But this part of our agreement. Everything's going to be alright.

COLE: Do I look alright? I was bleeding like a stuck pig out there.

DEE: Uh-oh. Marital strife!

KELLY: Will you shut the fuck up!
 COLE: Will you shut the fuck up!

DEE: (*trailing off*) You shut the fuck up...

ROLAND: Dee, Dee, Dee. Let's go, alright? Let them talk it out. I'm hungry. You hungry?

DEE: I could eat. I could definitely eat.

ROLAND: (*pause*) Okay, so, let's go!

DEE: Don't be rushing me motherfucker, I'll go when I'm damn good and ready.

Dee blows his nose. He puts a cigarette behind his ear.

DEE: Okay, I'm ready.

ROLAND: Jesus Christ, let's go.

Dee exits, but before Roland exits, he turns:

ROLAND: Feel better, Cole. See you soon, alright? Kelly, always a pleasure.

He exits. A long beat.

KELLY: You can't just up and walk away from the kind of money they're paying you.

COLE: Why not?

KELLY: (*to Cole*) Uh, there's things, there's the house, the car, the truck. Living! The debt we have! There's the future. Do you have a plan, something to do without these contracts?

COLE: I haven't decided. Even if I ended up leaving, I'll do something else.

KELLY: Okay. Like, what?

COLE: Fucking anything. Does it matter?

KELLY: Yes! Were you thinking about including me in this decision? I mean, it would be nice to have some sort of input so we can work these things out.

COLE: It's my decision to make.

KELLY: But it affects me too! These sorts of decisions affect me too!

COLE: You're working, we're not going to starve.

KELLY: Well, yeah, but...

COLE: But what?

KELLY: But...what if I lost the job, you know?

COLE: That's not even...Wait, you're not saying that you?..No fucking way.

KELLY: No...no, just--hey, just look at me. You know Lance?

COLE: Yes, I fucking know Lance. What the hell happened now?

KELLY: I told you we should've reported him when all this--

COLE: What happened?

KELLY: Well, they hired him back and he started doing the same crap as before and...I just lost it.

COLE: Oh, Christ...

KELLY: Yeah, I must've really laid into him. He lost a tooth.

DEE: Bitchin!

COLE: Jesus Christ. I mean, that's great but fuck...

KELLY: This is...this is fixable.

COLE: What does that mean? This is fucking insane.

KELLY: Well, that's the life you signed up for, sweetie. You can't just back out now.

COLE: I absolutely can. I can pull outta the contract for medical reasons. A guy at Aegis did it right before they folded.

KELLY: Okay, and then what? What happens then?

COLE: I don't know. You can find another job. I'll find another job. Anything. We'll figure something out. It will work itself out.

KELLY: I don't want this to sound like I'm putting this all on you, but *you* rented the house, the trucks and everything else that goes with it.

COLE: And all the student loans are yours. How much exactly?

KELLY: You know how much. That's not the point.

COLE: Oh, but it is. You just said that those things are mind and I'm telling you that the loan debt is yours.

KELLY: Fine. That is mine. But what are we going to do about the house and the truck and all that?

COLE: We'll return them.

KELLY: Return them? Are you kidding? (*beat*) Look, baby, I know, okay? I know you've been through an awful experience. I can't even begin to imagine the things you've seen ...or the things you've had to do. But remember the plan: a year. We just have to stick it out for a year and the house is ours -- that was the agreement. I'm here for you, baby.

COLE: You don't get it. You're not the one getting shot at; you can talk about agreements all day long. What does that even mean? It's bullshit: until you've been there and done the things I've done, you're just talking out of your ass.

KELLY: We had an agreement!

COLE: Fuck the agreement. Fuck this. Fuck the company. I'd rather work my hands to the bone digging goddamn ditches than go back there.

KELLY: You're just going to say, 'fuck it'? Is that right? Never mind that you're being paid ungodly amounts of money to do what you're good at. A year's worth of work and we'll have a house, a car and enough in the bank to be comfortable.

COLE: You don't understand.

KELLY: Then explain it to me.

COLE: I don't want to do it. Okay?

KELLY: So that's all the explanation I get?

Silence.

COLE: Is there something I don't do for you? I put myself out there, in the middle of this fucking hellhole; I bleed, I sweat, I watch people get blown apart. All for you. And it's not enough. And when I want to do something to get away from this...this shit, it comes back to you. What you want, what *you need*. You think I want a fucking house? I can live in a tent. You think I need that fucking car? I'll walk. That is, of course, if I don't get my fucking legs blown off first.

KELLY: This is *our* life--

COLE: This is *your* life! All this shit. All this bullshit. This is yours. *You* need it. I don't. And don't you look at me with that fucking face. That I'm-gonna-pout-like-a-fucking-child-face. I'm over it. This is all about you. It's always been about you.

KELLY: (*beat*) Wow...I just...whoa...

COLE: Yeah...well...

KELLY: Give me your hand.

Cole just looks at her.

KELLY: Give me your fucking hand, Cole.

He does. She places it on her belly.

KELLY: Surprise...it's not about you or me anymore.

COLE: Jesus...

KELLY: Wow.

COLE: (*pause*) How? I haven't been home in two-and-a-half months.

KELLY: I know.

COLE: (*long pause*) Is that baby mine?

KELLY: Of course it is!

COLE: I just want a yes.

KELLY: Yes! For god's sake, yes!

COLE: Yes, what?

KELLY: Yes, the baby is yours. What the hell is wrong with you?

COLE: Who was it?

KELLY: Who is what?

COLE: You know.

KELLY: There. Is. No. One. But. You. I love you.

COLE: (*long pause*) Why didn't you tell me about this when you first came in? Why did you wait until now?

KELLY: I wanted to. I tried to but Roland and

David--

COLE: His name is Dee.

KELLY: Okay, fine, whatever the hell he wants to call himself. Roland and Dee barged in and fucking ruined it. They came in here ranting and raving like crazy people. What was I supposed to do?

COLE: Interrupt those dip-shits. I don't know. Was it one of them?

KELLY: God, no! Not them!

COLE: So it was someone else!

KELLY: No...this is...no. I'm going to leave, get something to eat and then when I come back, hopefully you'll be feeling better. We can talk more about this when you're feeling better.

COLE: I'm fine.

KELLY: Regardless, I need some air...okay?

COLE: Well, let's not dally.

Kelly exits. Cole reaches over and grabs a bed-pan from underneath his bed. He vomits.

Lights down. The cast transitions into the scene and dress Cole in ratty sweats.

Scene Four.

Light's up on Daria's corner office with a view. New York City. Cole is alone. A beat. At the desk he flips through papers. He moves around the desk and tries opening the locked drawers. He goes through papers on her desk.

Daria enters.

DARIA: ...Sorry I'm late. (*stopping*) What are you doing?

COLE: (*befuddled*)....Uh, nothing. Sorry.

He moves around to the appropriate side of the desk. Daria takes her seat.

DARIA: Won't you have a seat?

COLE: No, I'm good.

DARIA: I have to insist.

COLE: No, I said.

DARIA: (beat) How are you healing, Cole?

COLE: Fine. We need to talk. It's important.

DARIA: I should hope so, you came all the way out here and called me at home to meet with you on a Saturday. What can I do for you, Mr. Hopkins?

COLE: I need, uh, I need a reassignment. I've had a death in my immediate family and I need to tend to certain, uh, details of the will and estate and so forth and I can't do that overseas. It's...impossible. Especially in Iraq or anywhere in the Middle East for that matter. It's just not, uh, feasible.

DARIA: Oh, wow. Oh, god. I'm sorry to hear that. My condolences.

COLE: Yeah. It's...it's a lot for us.

DARIA: May I ask who passed away?

COLE: Yeah. It's, uh, my wife's uncle.

DARIA: (pause) Hmmm?

COLE: Yeah, her uncle, uh, he was gardening and, uh, he seized up and they took him to the hospital and he had a aneurysm in his head the size of a fucking golf ball. Excuse me, the size of a golf ball. 24 hours later he was...kaput.

DARIA: I'm sorry, you said, 'your wife's uncle?'

COLE: Yeah.

DARIA: Well, I'm sorry but I can't tinker with a contract when a non-immediate family member dies. And your wife's uncle doesn't fall under the category of 'immediate family.'

COLE: Yeah, I realize that--

DARIA: You said he was immediate family.

COLE: Not for me. For my wife. This uncle raised her when her real father died.

DARIA: Uh-huh. What's his name?

COLE: Who's name?

DARIA: Her uncle's name.

COLE: Hal Ashby.

DARIA: Ashby? With a 'Y' or two 'EEs' or an 'IE'?

COLE: With a 'Y'.

Daria types a few things into her computer.

COLE: Yeah, so there's all sort um...

DARIA: (*typing*) Keep going, I'm listening.

COLE: There's all this sort of, you know, stuff -- legal stuff we've got to deal with. Or actually, *I* have to deal with it--

DARIA: Let me stop you right there. You said your wife's uncle, right? The one who raised her? Her father's dead, correct?

COLE: ...Yeah. Oh, yeah.

Daria turns her computer screen around to face Cole. It's open to Facebook; she points to a picture on the screen:

DARIA: Okay, if your wife's father's dead and he died when she was a child -- who's this in the picture on your wife's Facebook? And why does the caption say, "Me, my hubby..." -- that's you -- "...my mom and dad"? Hmmm? That's her uncle or her dad? Because the caption says it's her dad. See?

COLE: ...Well, that's...that's...that's her uncle, you see. She calls him dad but he's obviously not her dad. He's just...he is what he is...it's a weird family situation...(*small beat*) Does that make sense? Let me know if I'm being unclear. Sometimes I tend to gloss over things.

DARIA: So what? Her mother married her uncle? Like Hamlet? Is this --? I'm confused.

COLE: (*long pause*) Yes.

DARIA: Okay. Listen, Cole: I don't like liars. I have thoroughly vetted you and your family and your wife's father isn't dead, he's 62 years old and living in Chico, California. I can tell you his address if you'd like. And her uncle is very much alive. In fact, according to this, he was first place in the 60-and-older category in the Ironman Triathlon...yesterday. So how about you stop lying to me and tell me why you're really here?

COLE: ...He died yesterday.

DARIA: Cole, he did not. If you want to keep playing these games with me, I'm gonna have to ask you to leave.

COLE: I know it *seems* like the truth is being muddled here...but trust me, he's dead.

DARIA: (*beat; rising*) Alright, you're going to have to leave.

COLE: Just let me clarify this.

DARIA: Leave! Get back on a plane and get back to your team and your station.

COLE: No.

DARIA: No?

COLE: No, I can't. That's not an option. I can't finish the contract. It's just not possible.

DARIA: What does that mean? Explain that to me.

COLE: It means I can't, okay?

DARIA: You can't or you won't?

COLE: I won't. I can't.

DARIA: (*beat*) Okay, I'll bite: why?

COLE: You won't understand. It doesn't matter.

DARIA: How do you know I wouldn't understand? I think it does matter.

COLE: It's personal. It's very personal. It has nothing to do with anything. It's just...me. Okay?

DARIA: So, because of this 'personal issue' that has nothing to do with anything, you can't go back and complete your contract. Is that right?

COLE: ...It's bigger than that.

DARIA: Listen: I'm gonna be straight with you. If you're not back at your post in Iraq within 24 hours, I will take this matter to our in-house counsel and they will handle from there. And when I mean, they'll handle it, I mean they will start legal proceedings against you for breaking your contract and eventually they will win and they will take you for everything you've got and then some. They've got this down to a science. So, what's it gonna be? Play ball or not play ball -- it's up to you.

COLE: (*a long beat*) Have you ever been in combat? Huh? (*beat*) You stink. You stink, you know that? You fucking REMFs, you Rear-Echelon MotherFuckers all have the same smell: the smell of bullshit. You sit back here on your fucking high-horse of judgment and talk down to me like I'm the fucking help. You don't know what it's like to do this. A piece of metal the size of a fingernail was this far away from my fucking spine. I could reach into my own head and touch the bottom of my skull. What the fuck have you done, you fucking pencil-pusher.

DARIA: (*pause*) Mr. Hopkins, you asked if I've ever seen combat.

COLE: I'm sorry?

DARIA: No, it's okay. You let it out. But let me answer your question as thoroughly as I possibly can. I served with the 82nd Airborne during three different deployments in Iraq and Afghanistan. More to the point I think you're trying to make: we were ambushed in Mosul, Iraq. This is 2005. An IED goes off. It knocks me around enough that I black-out. When I come to, I'm being dragged away from the Humvee, through the streets. I thought, oh great, my guys are taking care of me. No, it was two Iraqis -- insurgents. I'm bleeding and I can't hear a thing, let alone fight back. I black-out again. I wake up in some fucking dungeon in the middle of god-knows-where. I'm tied up. Oh, and I didn't mention that I can -- could -- speak some Arabic. It's dark and all I can hear is this argument between two of the insurgents happening in the next room. I couldn't tell you what exactly what was being said but the gist of it was that they were discussing whether or not it would be 'politically relevant' to just simply kill me or keep me alive and...do whatever they wanted to do to me until they could negotiate something with my commanders...

Daria lifts her sleeve, revealing a dense web of scars covering her arm; apparently, the insurgents tried to skin her alive, beginning with her arms...

DARIA: They settled for something in the middle.

COLE: Shit.

DARIA: So when you tell me, 'you can't do this,' I have just four words for you: man-the-fuck-up. You have responsibilities. Learn them. Love them. Be grateful; there's a lot of people who are much worse off than you. And who, by the way, are doing a much better job than you.

COLE: A better job? What's that mean?

DARIA: Exactly what it sounds like. Some of the reports from your superiors in the company--(*she pulls out a binder and opens it*)--state that your marksmanship scores have been dipping lower and lower down to just a touch above the minimum. They also complain that you lack motivation and drive to complete assignments. In addition, we've had several reports circulating the company that the attack on your team and your injuries could have been avoided if you'd taken the proper precautions, if you'd been in radio contact with the rest of your team, if you'd followed one item of the company's protocol.

COLE: You don't know that. There's no possible way...with all that shit going on, no rational person can say what would or would not have happened. That's a stupid thing to say. You can never know what the fuck would have happened.

DARIA: Well, I'll tell you what I do know: you just sat there and told me your wife's Ironman-Triathlon-completing uncle died yesterday so you can get out of your pricey contract. Look at me: what is going on with you?

COLE: (*pause*) I'm scared...shitless. I'm terrified. That little piece of metal was so close to my spine. You just can't imagine.

DARIA: You said that. Yes, I can imagine but here's the deal: you're not some minimum wage security guard standing outside a bank who has the option of running away when a man with a gun shows up to knock the place over. You don't have that option and you want to know why? Hmmm? Because we're in the process of paying you $86,000 to protect people, places and transports in Iraq. Not to mention the significant bump in pay we gave you to help cover any unforeseen costs your medical treatment might incur. We're not paying you be scared. And we're certainly not paying you to come here to bitch and moan about it. You want to know what I think? Fuck your fear. Grow up and grow a pair of balls. Get up, suit up and get out there and do what you gotta do.

COLE: But I'm...

DARIA: Is there anything else I can help you with?

COLE: No.

DARIA: Good. I'm going home. You know where this company stands and you know where I stand. I hope you'll make right decision and get back on a plane.

With that, Cole rises and exits, leaving Daira alone. A long beat.

She presses a button on her office phone:

DARIA: Melissa, can you get me Dr. Portia Ellis' number? Thank you.

Lights down. The next scene is set by the rest of the cast and Cole is dressed into his 'contractor gear' -- weapons, ammunition, cap, sunglasses, etc.

Scene Five.

Lights up. Trustwell Security Solutions Compound -- Mosul, Iraq. Common Area. A sign on the wall reads: "Firearm safeties must always be engaged while in this building. Any employee found without their safety engaged are liable to be subject to disciplinary action. Thank you, Management -- Trustwell Security Solutions."

Cole laces up his shoes.

Dr. Portia Ellis enters.

DR. ELLIS: Mr. Hopkins?

COLE: Yeah.

DR. ELLIS: Cole Hopkins?

COLE: Yes. That's me.

DR. ELLIS: (*shakes his hand*) Doctor Portia Ellis. Daria Kandt in New York sent me to talk to you. You got a minute?

COLE: Yeah. You came all the way from New York?

DR. ELLIS: Well, I have office space in London but I like to make house calls like this.

COLE: What kind of doctor are you?

DR. ELLIS: A psychiatrist.

COLE: Oh, yeah?

DR. ELLIS: You're a hard man to nail down. I went by your quarters and talked to four people before I thought to look for you in here.

COLE: Well, here I am. (*like Bugs Bunny*)What's up, Doc?

DR. ELLIS: That never gets old.

COLE: We gotta make this quick. I got some place to be.

DR. ELLIS: We'll keep it brief.

COLE: What can I do for you?

DR. ELLIS: I wanted to see how you were doing.

COLE: I'm great. That all?

DR. ELLIS: I'm asking about how you feel.

COLE: I feel great.

DR. ELLIS: Do you?

COLE: I'll live. A little sleeplessness but that should sort itself out.

DR. ELLIS: How much sleep you have been missing?

COLE: I didn't sleep last night.

DR. ELLIS: Anxious?

COLE: You could say that.

DR. ELLIS: Anxious about being back?

COLE: Who wouldn't be?

DR. ELLIS: There's no judgment in my questions. What specifically makes you anxious?

COLE: Anxious is the wrong word. It's more like...excited.

DR. ELLIS: You like being back in Iraq?

COLE: (*pause*) I gotta go. There's a shipment going out and I gotta be riding shotgun.

DR. ELLIS: I talked to management. They're pushing the departure time back another hour.

COLE: Oh. Alright.

DR. ELLIS: May I ask, why didn't you take some time off after you were released from the hospital in Germany? I understand that you made a stop in New York at the company's offices. But that only lasted a day. Why not take a vacation. Get a massage. You have a family, right?

COLE: Uh-huh.

DR. ELLIS: You could've spent some time with them. Relax. Why didn't you do that?

COLE: That's a no-go, Doc.

DR. ELLIS: May I ask why?

COLE: Why do you care?

DR. ELLIS: It's my job to care. What was going through your head? Indulge me.

COLE: Okay. There's a rhythm to things, you know?

DR. ELLIS: That's interesting...

COLE: A momentum. And you just don't stop a momentum once it gets going. You know what that is? It's a car going sixty miles per hour and colliding with a piece on concrete. You can't do that.

DR. ELLIS: You're in a momentum.

COLE: Yeah. I gotta keep it going, you know?

DR. ELLIS: Is that why you came back to Iraq?

COLE: My god, it has everything to do with it. If I go home, I'll get into that momentum and that momentum is dangerous. After two days I'll feel like an elephant is stepping on my chest. I'll start drinking and pissing the wrong people off.

DR. ELLIS: Can I offer an opinion?

COLE: No one's stopping you.

DR. ELLIS: I think what you're describing as a 'momentum' is actually some form of an addiction. Now hear me out, this is not uncommon.

COLE: What?

DR. ELLIS: You do know what Post-Traumatic Stress is?

COLE: Ah, what the fuck? Really? You're gonna start with this shit now?

DR. ELLIS: From what you've told me, these symptoms, this need to constantly--

COLE: I didn't say 'constantly.'

DR. ELLIS: You didn't let me finish. Your need to constantly seek some form of excitement, some action, that's a very prominent symptom of P.T.S.D.

COLE: Jesus Christ, doc. I'm just trying to make some money and not get bored off my tit. That's all.

Any more than that, you're just reading way too much into shit.

DR. ELLIS: Then what is the 'momentum' you're talking about?

COLE: (*pause*) Are you talking to Roland about this kinda shit? To Dee?

DR. ELLIS: I'm just asking questions. But I will say that there have been some concerns about your behavior.

COLE: From who?

DR. ELLIS: Well, I can say that your wife contacted Daria Kandt with her concerns. They're very real concerns.

COLE: Un-fucking-believable. You guys...

Cole moves to leave...

DR. ELLIS: But I have to tell you: if you leave before we conclude this interview, it will be reflected in the final report. This final report will be sent to Trustwell Security Solutions.

COLE: My wife was talking to her about *my* behavior?

DR. ELLIS: That's right. Then Daria came to me.

COLE: And now you're here. Great. Just fucking great. Well, you tell them...

DR. ELLIS: What?

COLE: Never mind.

DR. ELLIS: We can do this another time.

COLE: Lets.

Cole exits. Lights down.

Scene Six.

Lights up. Rooftop, Trustwell Security Compound -- Mosul, Iraq. Two weeks later.

Amongst the satellite dishes and antenna, three pool chaises are set up facing down-stage. A shirtless Cole lies face-up on the middle chaise, sunbathing. Between the hatch and the row of chaises is a large Coleman cooler. Up-stage of the chaises is a metal hatch leading down into the compound. Cole's shirt, shoes, hat, web gear, and weapon lie strewn about the rooftop, as if they were ripped off violently and thrown away.

A beat. Cole sips his beer. He wears a sidearm in a holster.

Off-stage, a tinny radio can be heard. It gets louder until the up-stage hatch flies open. Dee climbs out holding a portable speaker wired to his iPod. An obnoxious tune like "Angel with a Shotgun" by The Cab or "Naturally" by Selena Gomez and the Scene blasts from the portable speaker.

<u>DEE</u>: (*noticing Cole*) Whoa, ho, ho! My brother from another mother!

Dee dances over to Cole.

<u>DEE</u>: Come on, dance with me motherfucka!

<u>COLE</u>: Shut up.

DEE: What?

COLE: What do you want?

DEE: What?

COLE: I said, what do you want?

DEE: What?

COLE: I said, turn that fucking thing off.

DEE: (*turning it off*) Sorry, brah.

Dee peels off his shirt and takes a seat on one of the chaises. A long beat.

DEE: It's dry as a motherfucker out here! Wooo! (*pause*) Have you ever noticed that, like, 99.99% of Iraqis have mustaches...even the women? They all look like someone's creepy uncle. It's fucking Pedo-Land. (*pause*) I said, it's fucking Pedophile-Land. Man, that's funny. (pause) Good beer, dude. What is this, domestic? (*pause*) I'm going to break into your room tonight when you're sleeping and shit on your head. I'm dead serious.

COLE: (*long pause*) Yep.

DEE: Fuck it. I don't know why I even bother with this shit. (*pause*) You're better off here, you know that right? Stick to what you know, that's what I always say. I mean, what are you gonna do? Work construction? Drive a minivan? Have a house with a nice white picket fence?

COLE: That sounds nice.

DEE: That sounds gay! You're a warrior, man. A Ranger, baby -- HOO-AHH! Not some fucking sheep. We live it, man. Other people talk about it. We live it. There's no bullshit out here, man. It's pure. Someone gets fucking uppity and starts waving their fucking weapon in your face, you put that motherfucker down. Clean. Primal. Fuck, I love it! By the way, how's Kelly doing?

COLE: She's fine.

DEE: And the baby?

COLE: I don't know.

DEE: Okay. That's kinda weird, don't you think?

COLE: I don't know. You want another beer?

DEE: Hell yeah! Can you get it for me, bro? I'm starting to feel the sizzle.

COLE: Ugh. Really?

DEE: Yeah, dude, I'm comfortable. Do me a solid.

COLE: Don't be throwing those empty cans off the roof anymore. And don't be pissing off the roof also. The guards have been complaining. Use a fucking toilet like a human being.

DEE: You sound like my mom.

COLE: You have a mother? I thought you were the spawn of Satan.

DEE: She says the same thing! But no, my mother's actually a very nice person; she gets the hot flashes now and again. I'll come home and the house will be a fucking freezer and I gotta say, "Hey, mom, that's shit's in your head." She doesn't believe. What are you gonna do?

Cole gets up, retrieves a beer from the cooler and hands it to Dee. Cole has deep bleeding fingernail scratches under his arms, along his ribs.

DEE: (*re: the scratches*) Whoa, shit, what the hell is that?

COLE: It's just an accident...

DEE: No, I get that. A wound from what? What were you, fighting Freddy Krueger or some shit?

COLE: No.

DEE: Dude, those are nasty looking.

COLE: It's fine.

DEE: Dude, they're fucking bleeding.

COLE: Moving around must've caused them to reopen.

DEE: No shit, ya think? You need to get that checked out.

COLE: I said, it's fine. Go back to your fucking beer.

DEE: (*pause*) Are those scratches? What did that? Did you do that to yourself? (*pause*)You know I wouldn't really shit on your head? You know that, right?

COLE: I know that, Dee. That's not the problem.

DEE: You're damn right it's not a problem. It never will be.

COLE: (*beat*) Is it hard to keep all this up?

DEE: What?

COLE: All this bullshit you put on. All crazy guy shit. Does it exhaust you?

DEE: What the hell are you talking about?

COLE: So you're really this stupid and careless?

DEE: Whoa! What the fuck? Where is this coming

from?

COLE: It's coming from: I'm tired of you and your mouth. Can you shut up for five seconds?

DEE: Fuck you, man!

COLE: Can you? Can you just stop with the inane comments for one minute? For just one minute? Can you do that?

DEE: What does that mean? What does 'inane' mean? Is that more of your faggot liberal bullshit? Huh?

COLE: My god, you're a fucking disaster.

DEE: I'm a disaster? I'm a fucking disaster? Look at you, you fucking mook: you get wounded and you think the sky is falling. "Oh my god, oh my god. I didn't realize how dangerous war is." Dude, really? You don't shave, you don't shower, you're lagging behind all the goddamn time. And when you are caught up, you're like a fucking zombie. Now you got all these scratches on you. You did that shit to yourself, didn't you?

COLE: Just go. I was having a good day--

DEE: Were you? Dude, you're bleeding all over the fucking chaise.

COLE: I was having a good day until you came up

here and started bothering me with your music and your nonsense.

DEE: Who are you? Who do you think you are? What is so goddamn important that I can't talk to you for five minutes? You're slipping, Cole. No one else has the balls to say it, but you're the goddamn disaster here. I haven't been able to get five fucking words out of you since you came back. And then you're flying off the handle at me because I have the nerve to talk to you, be friendly with you. Why the fuck am I still here talking to you? Fuck this shit. I tried to help but you wanted to be Mister Dramatic Cutter over here and bleed all over my chaises; that's right, *my* chaises! You know what? Get the fuck up, get off my chaise!

COLE: Or what?

DEE: I'll slap you with my dick.

COLE: You make a move on me, man, I'll draw on you.

DEE: The fuck you will.

COLE: The fuck I won't.

DEE: Man, I ought to slap you with my dick just to knock some sense into you.

COLE: (*placing his hand on his gun*) Make a move.

DEE: The hell are you doing?

COLE: Make a fucking move.

DEE: I was kidding. Is this how you act around Kelly?

Cole draws his sidearm.

COLE: The fuck did you just say?

DEE: Okay. I'm...let's just breathe here.

COLE: Listen to me. Are you listening?

DEE: I'm all ears.

COLE: Good. I put up with a lot of shit from a lot of people.

DEE: Who? Who gives you shit?

COLE: The fucking...You, Daria, Roland...and Kelly. I just want to be left alone. If I gotta be here in this...shit-hole, I want to be left alone. If I want to sit up here and drink my fucking beer in peace, I'm going to sit up here and drink my fucking beer in peace and not you or some other mongoloid is going to interrupt me. Does that compute? Am I being clear?

DEE: Crystal.

COLE: Good.

DEE: (*pause*) You want to put your sidearm away?

COLE: Oh.

Cole holsters his pistol.

Dee collects his things and heads for the hatch. He stops.

DEE: Call your wife. I don't know what's going on but she's been writing all kinds of emails and I guess she's been calling the office nonstop. I think you need to call her. And that's...that.

Dee exits. Cole stands alone.

Lights down. The rest of the cast changes the scene; Kelly dresses Cole:

Scene Seven.

Lights up on the Stage-Left half of the stage. Cole's cramped quarters -- Trustwell Security Compound -- Mosul, Iraq. A twin bed, small desk and swivel chair make up the entirety of the room's furniture. The walls of the space have angry, violent handwritten graffiti scrawled in diagonal arcs across the wall. Accenting the graffiti are fist-sized holes punched in the drywall -- some have flakes of blood around the rims of the holes.

Cole sits at the desk with his laptop open. A beat. He stares at the laptop then out of the blue, he presses some buttons....

Lights up on the Stage-Right half of the stage. A middle-class living room. San Diego, California. A dining room table, framed pictures on the wall and a vase of fresh flowers stand in stark contrast to the bug-hole that Cole lives in. On the dining room table sits an open laptop. The laptop chirps with an incoming Skype call. Kelly enters; she is about three months along (and showing). She pauses then sits and answers the call.

<u>KELLY</u>: Hey. (*pause*) How are you?

<u>COLE</u>: I'm well. I guess. It's been too long.

<u>KELLY</u>: Yeah. You don't say.

<u>COLE</u>: And I've been purposefully avoiding

making this call.

KELLY: I figured. Or answering my emails.

COLE: Or answering your emails.

KELLY: Or answering my letters.

COLE: Or answering your letters.

KELLY: Or making one effort to--

COLE: I get it. I get it. I'm sorry. I'm fucked up. I don't know how else to say it. I have this weight on me all the time. I hate this fucking place. I'm sorry, I'm bitching and rambling. How are you? Can I see it?

KELLY: You mean, the baby?

COLE: Yeah.

KELLY: You really want to see my fat belly?

COLE: More than anything.

KELLY: Alright. Here we go.

She stands and lifts her shirt, revealing her pregnant baby-belly.

COLE: Wow...that's amazing. How are you feeling?

KELLY: I'm good, Cole. I missed you.

COLE: I missed you too and I'm sorry about everything. I'm so fucked up, I don't even realize how badly some of the things I've said hurt you. And I'm sorry I didn't get back to you sooner. Is there any way you can forgive me?

KELLY: (*pause*) Cole...

COLE: I mean, I know I really messed up here but I'm willing to do whatever it takes to make this right.

KELLY: Cole...

COLE: I love you Kelly and I care about this. Please.

KELLY: Cole, I need you to listen.

COLE: Anything.

KELLY: I need you to listen to me very carefully.

COLE: Okay, I'm listening.

KELLY: Oh, god...

COLE: It's okay, I'm here, I'm listening.

KELLY: I really don't know how to say this.

COLE: Best way I know is to just say it.

KELLY: I think that...

COLE: Yes!

KELLY: Oh God, I think this baby isn't yours.

COLE: (*pause*) What?

KELLY: I don't think this baby's yours. It's not yours. There's no way.

COLE: No, I fucking heard you. I'm just...

KELLY: I'm sorry. I'm so sorry, Cole. It doesn't have to be this way.

COLE: I just...what? (*pause*) Who? Who?

KELLY: (*pause*) You know him.

COLE: Lance. Jesus-fucking-Christ.

KELLY: I'm sorry.

COLE: You're fucking with me, aren't you? This is fucking joke. It has to be.

KELLY: I'm sorry.

COLE: No. Did...did I do something? WHAT THE FUCK?! What is this?

KELLY: I'm sorry.

COLE: Is that all you can say, 'I'm sorry'? What the fuck does that...never mind. Do you love me? Or better yet, have you ever loved me? Is all this just some kind of game and I'm the loser here? The sucker?

KELLY: No.

COLE: Because it sure seems that way. How? How did this happen? Did he force you? Was it like that?

KELLY: No, Cole. It wasn't like that.

COLE: You gotta give me something here. A shred of something to work with. Anything.

KELLY: Cole, look at me. Please look at me.

COLE: I'm looking.

KELLY: I love you more than anything else in the world.

COLE: Oh, god.

KELLY: No, please hear me. I do love you.

COLE: You know what? That's sick. That's fucking sick. Who says that? "I love you." After they've done something like this?

KELLY: What did you expect me to say?

COLE: I don't know. Anything. Just not that. "I love you." Fuck.

A long beat between them.

KELLY: I do love you.

COLE: God, fuck you. I just want to know, how do you rationalize this? Because I know you're fucking master at rationalizing all your bullshit. Huh? What is your fucking excuse now?

KELLY: (*pause*) There is none. There is no excuse for what I've done. You're right. You're absolutely, one hundred percent right.

COLE: Don't patronize me.

KELLY: I'm not. I swear I'm not.

COLE: Good.

KELLY: I know you're angry.

COLE: No shit.

KELLY: What do we do now?

COLE: *We* don't do shit. *We* are over. Like I said, *you* can go fuck yourself. And as far as that kid...it's a weight off my shoulders, I'll tell you that. You go play house with that fucking moron and his fucking moron kid. You two deserve each other, you fucking whore. I just hope for your sake-- (*pointing at her belly*)--and for his sake, it was worth it. Have fun.

<u>KELLY</u>: I'm sorry, Cole.

<u>COLE</u>: Jesus, just shut up.

Cole presses a button on his laptop and Kelly's half of the stage is blacked out. He picks up his laptop and smashes it to bits against the desk. A beat. Lights down. The cast returns to clear and set the stage for the next scene -- placing each weapon or vest individually. Cole disappears:

Scene Eight.

Lights up. Trustwell Security Compound. Rooftop. All sorts of guns, ammunition and other armaments lay strewn about the rooftop. Rifles, submachine guns, and handguns are lined up according to make and size. Boxes of ammunition are stacked according to caliber, regular and armor-piercing. Kevlar vests are arranged largest to smallest. It's enough weapons, ammunition and armor to outfit a small army.

The hatch opens and Cole enters carrying a high powered rifle. He sets it amongst the others and begins to count his "stock". He produces a small notepad and begins taking down the count. A beat.

<u>COLE:</u> (*to himself, writing*) Armor-piercing 9mm -- three crates. Two full, one approximately half full.

Roland enters through the hatch, looks around and stops.

<u>ROLAND:</u> (*to himself*) Jesus Christ...(*to Cole*) Cole, my man, how goes it?

<u>COLE:</u> Fine.

<u>ROLAND:</u> (*re: the armaments*)You got them all out again. Great. Can I ask you something?

<u>COLE:</u> Shoot.

ROLAND: Why are they all out again?

COLE: They need to be counted regularly and it's not being taken care of on any level.

ROLAND: You counted them all yesterday.

COLE: It's not safe.

ROLAND: And they're safe up here?

COLE: How many warning shots did Dee fire yesterday during the convoy? Ten? Fifteen?

ROLAND: I don't know. You're doing this because of safety?

COLE: Like I said, I'm counting them. There are all sorts of fucking--I don't need to tell you--the shifty motherfuckers we got roaming around here. And I'm not even talking about the Iraqis. That's a whole other story. Those fuckers will steal anything not bolted down. I'm talking about keeping order, keeping track of all this shit so when something does go wrong we have a record. Is something about this out of line?

ROLAND: Today is your day off.

COLE: There are no days off here, Roland. You know that.

ROLAND: Do you know how the locks on Jimmy

and Dee's room where broken?

COLE: Like I said, all sorts of shifty motherfuckers around here.

ROLAND: Did you break the locks to get to their stuff and then bring it up here?

COLE: Nah, man. This shit was out. I didn't break anything.

Roland picks up a vest.

ROLAND: (*reading*) "Dee." This is Dee's vest. Cole, look at me: what'd you do?

COLE: Nothing, man. It was laying out.

ROLAND: Alright, you need to stop this. Seriously. You've been scavenging people's equipment and dragging it up here every day this week. Nobody can find a rifle or a vest when they need it because you're up here logging them or whatever the hell you're doing. I don't know if you realize this but you're actually making the place more unsafe by keeping all this shit up here. (*beat*) You've counted it. Great. And now you need to put all this shit back and stop taking it out and counting it every day.

COLE: Why?

ROLAND: Because it's not normal. And like I said you're putting this whole operation in danger. We need this equipment.

COLE: I can appreciate that.

ROLAND: Then put it back. Now. Alright? Let's go.

COLE: Don't touch anything. I'm not finished yet.

ROLAND: No, no, no. You're done here. Let's pack it up. I'll help you.

COLE: I said, don't touch anything.

ROLAND: (*pause*) Alright, you're going to pack all this up and take back down to the armory and never touch any of it again. Is that understood?

COLE: Yeah, sure.

ROLAND: Don't fuck with me on this, man. Alright? Now, let's get moving.

COLE: Do not touch a single fucking thing on this roof. I'm counting.

ROLAND: You're not doing shit!

COLE: I don't come to your post and tell you how to do your job, do I?

ROLAND: This is not a matter of whose job is what. I'm going to say this for the third time -- what you're doing is putting the rest of us in danger. If you can't see that, if you can't at least understand what I'm talking about: that's a problem.

COLE: There's no problem here. I'm doing my work and you're interrupting that work.

ROLAND: Who told you to do this?

COLE: It needs to get done and it's not getting done. It's as simple as that.

ROLAND: Alright, we can keep going around and around in circles with this shit. You need to come down off this roof--

Roland approaches Cole and tries to guide him off the roof.

COLE: Don't touch me! Get your fucking hands off me. I'm warning you.

ROLAND: Or what?

COLE: Or I'm gonna throw you off this roof.

ROLAND: What is going on with you? Why are you like this?

COLE: Like what?

ROLAND: Like being obsessed with this shit.

COLE: It's my job.

ROLAND: No, see, it's not your job; it's never been your job and I don't recall anyone ever assigning this to you.

COLE: It needs to get done.

ROLAND: Listen, I'm not gonna stand here and argue--

An off-stage explosion rocks Roland and Cole.

ROLAND: Holy shit! Where was that?

Small arms fire begins off-stage. Sirens blare.

COLE: (*pointing*): Right over there. See it? The north gate.

ROLAND: Oh, shit. We gotta go. (*looking around at the armaments and gear*) Oh, fuck. This is what I'm talking about! Grab what you need and let's go. We'll have to let everyone know that their gear is up here. Come on!

They grab weapons and ammunition and whatever else they can carry. They exit through the hatch. Lights down. The small arms fire continues through the transition until the next scene begins. The cast tucks the weapons and vests away; they set the scene:

THE WAR MACHINE

Scene Nine.

Lights up. Common Area. Trustwell Security Solutions -- Mosul, Iraq. Two hours later.

Dee and Roland enter. They are exhausted and filthy -- they've had a motherfucker of a day.

DEE: What do we do?

ROLAND: I don't know.

DEE: Cigarette?

ROLAND: No. Thank you.

Dee lights a cigarette.

ROLAND: I keep thinking about Kelly and how we're going to tell her.

DEE: That's not our job. That's the company's job.

ROLAND: I know that. I just feel like we should be the ones to tell her. Not some dick in a suit. Some stranger on the phone. That's not fair to anyone; I don't care what they've done.

DEE: We shouldn't get in the middle of it. Besides, we don't know if he's dead. We don't know what the hell happened. I mean, he could be hiding for all we know.

ROLAND: We searched every inch of this place. I was ankle-deep sifting through garbage. We have looked everywhere. There is physically nowhere else he can be. Not in the base.

DEE: I'm just trying to be one of those 'glass half full' people. That's all. That fact is: we don't know.

ROLAND: Let's just be clear: what did you see? Let's be clear about what we saw.

DEE: Alright. I'm eating...a Power Bar? I don't know.

ROLAND: It doesn't matter.

DEE: I hear the 'boom' and I didn't have my piece. I have to run up to the roof and grab my piece after Cole put all that shit up there. What the fuck was that, by the way?

ROLAND: I don't want to get into it.

DEE: Alright. I make it out to the north gate, which is on fire.

ROLAND: Yeah, I saw that and I saw you.

DEE: And I see Jimmy and Bill laying down some fire on one of the far buildings. I start peppering the building. I don't know what the fuck's going on. Bill and Jimmy don't know what the fuck's going on. We're all choking on smoke from the burning cars.

ROLAND: When did you see Cole?

DEE: He was already there. He was closer to the building we were shooting at. He was in cover behind one of the Kyocera containers.

ROLAND: I was behind the sandbags.

DEE: Which ones?

ROLAND: To the east. We were getting choked with smoke too.

DEE: So in the middle of all this I see Cole break cover head to that car that got all shot to shit.

ROLAND: Everyone was dead, right? In the car? The white Mercedes?

DEE: Is that what it was? Everybody had to be dead as door nails. There's no way. You saw it. There must've been two thousand holes in that car. We shot the hell out of it. And you could see the bodies in here getting shot to pieces.

ROLAND: Then what?

DEE: He makes it to the car and, I don't know, I couldn't see what he was doing but I could tell he was fucking around in the car.

ROLAND: He was inside the car?

DEE: For a solid two minutes. Maybe more.

ROLAND: I think that's when I headed back to re-arm.

DEE: Probably. I moved forward and sent the word down the line that we had a friendly in that car. I looked back and he was gone.

ROLAND: Gone?

DEE: Yeah. He was there and then he wasn't.

ROLAND: Are you're sure he was there in the first place.

DEE: Yes! It was him. I could tell by that ugly fucking cap he wears.

ROLAND: Did he say what he was doing out there in the car as we were shooting the shit outta it?

DEE: I didn't talk to Cole. I don't think anybody did. He was just there by himself.

Cole's guttural scream is heard.

COLE: (*off*) Get off me, motherfucker! Get your--I said, get off me! You want to fuck with me? Huh!? Back the fuck up!

DEE: (*to Roland*) No fucking way.

ROLAND: Shit.

DEE: It sounds like him.

ROLAND: It's him.

Cole enters and locks the door behind him. His arms and chest are covered in blood -- he is filthy. He holds his rifle at the ready. He wears a back pack on his back.

COLE: (*calling off*)You're not coming in!

VOICES: (*off*) Open the door, Cole.

COLE: (*calling off*) I'm gonna put holes in this door if you don't step the fuck away!

VOICES: (*off*) Alright, Cole. We're stepping away.

COLE: (*calling off*) Now get lost. I need to be alone. You hear me? Fuck off! I don't want to hear you scratching around the door. Or else I'm gonna empty this entire motherfucking mag into this door!

DEE: Hey, Cole.

COLE: (*turning*) Jesus-fucking-Christ! What the hell? What are you guys doing in here?

DEE: What's up?

COLE: What?

DEE: I said, what's up. You good?

ROLAND: You alright, Cole? You need to see a medic?

COLE: No, I need...I need...I don't know what I need. Step back.

DEE: Okay.

ROLAND: (*to Cole*) You want to sit down? Take off some of that gear?

COLE: Okay.

ROLAND: Where the hell have you been, man? We've been looking everywhere. I was knee-deep in shit looking for you.

COLE: I was out. I was doing some work.

ROLAND: What kind of work? You had the whole base looking for you.

COLE: Important work.

DEE: Yeah?

COLE: Yeah. I think I want to be alone.

ROLAND: Is that right?

COLE: Yeah, I think need to have some time for

myself. Just...

ROLAND: I don't think that's a good idea.

COLE: I didn't ask you what you think. I said, I want to be alone.

DEE: You actually said, you *thought* you wanted to be alone.

COLE: I want to be alone.

ROLAND: We're not leaving you alone. That's out of the question. You need to sit down, take off your shit and just relax.

A beat. Cole sits. He sets his back pack down.

ROLAND: There you go, man.

Cole peals off layers of gear.

ROLAND: What's going on, man. Where did this blood come from?

COLE: Oh, you know...

ROLAND: No, I don't.

COLE: Gimme a cigarette.

Roland gives Cole a cigarette.

COLE: A light.

Dee lights Cole's cigarette. A beat.

COLE: Do you ever just wish the chatter in your head would stop?

ROLAND: What?

COLE: Quieting the mind. Do you ever wish you could stop it?

ROLAND: Sure. Who wouldn't want a zen moment or two. But I'm not sure if that's totally possible.

COLE: Oh, it's possible. Totally possible. Thoroughly possible.

ROLAND: You've experienced that?

COLE: Yeah, twice. The first time when I was getting my wisdom teeth out and the dentist gave me a monster dose of Valium to calm my nerves. I didn't give fuck. I was doing a standup comedy routine in the waiting room. I had the whole room cracking up. It was a good time.

ROLAND: And the second time?

COLE: (*pause*) Today.

ROLAND: Oh. During the firefight?

COLE: Yep.

ROLAND: Well, why are you covered in blood?

COLE: It's war paint, bro.

ROLAND: It's blood.

COLE: Suit yourself.

ROLAND: Can you tell us where you've been?

COLE: If I tell you, will you leave alone? Just let me sit here?

DEE: Totally.

ROLAND: Let's hear it.

COLE: (*pause*) I consider both of you my brothers. You know that, right? And brothers don't rat on brothers, right?

ROLAND: Yeah.

DEE: Nice!

COLE: If I show you guys something, you can't tell anyone about it. And if I tell you where I've been, you won't say anything.

ROLAND: Sure.

DEE: Mum's the word.

COLE: Promise you won't tell anyone.

DEE: I promise. What is it?

ROLAND: Sure.

COLE: Promise me, Roland.

ROLAND: I promise I won't tell anyone. What is it?

Cole opens his back pack and removes a severed human head -- a young Iraqi's head.

ROLAND: Oh, shit! Jesus-fucking-Christ!

DEE: Jesus-shit! Oh my god! Oh my god! What the fuck?

ROLAND: What the fuck is that? What the fuck are you doing with that? Oh, god. Oh, god.

DEE: I'm gonna be fucking sick.

COLE: Don't you puke in here.

DEE: Fuck you!

ROLAND: Where the hell did you get that from?

COLE: I took it.

ROLAND: (*pause*) Where did you take it from?

COLE: A car.

ROLAND: Was it outside the gates?

COLE: Yeah.

ROLAND: Did you find the head like this? Cut off?

COLE: No.

ROLAND: You cut it off.

COLE: Uh-huh.

ROLAND: Why? Why the fuck would you do something like that?

COLE: We're here to win, right?

ROLAND: Is that a question?

COLE: I'm serious.

ROLAND: So am I. What are you asking here?

COLE: Are we here to win this war?

ROLAND: No, we're here to guard what they tell us to guard. That's all. The job of winning this motherfucker is the Army, Navy and Marines' job. We get paid to guard people, places and things. We are not paid to conduct offensive operations. And we are certainly not paid to do this kind of shit.

COLE: Come on. We do offensive stuff all the time when shit gets unhinged. You've raided houses right along with the Marines. Don't give me that shit about how we never do it.

ROLAND: But it's not our job. This is not our job. This is sick. You are broken, my friend.

COLE: Broken huh?

DEE: Yeah.

COLE: (*to Dee*) I don't remember asking your opinion.

ROLAND: It's sick. This is a problem.

COLE: It's necessary.

ROLAND: Nothing like this is ever necessary. What are you? Fucking Ghengis Khan? Cutting off heads like some conqueror of old?

COLE: It's necessary. For me.

ROLAND: How? What does that mean? How in the fuck...How? I just want to know what you're thinking. What's going on in there?

COLE: I don't think you'll understand.

ROLAND: Well, do you mind fucking enlightening us to this new-found fucking wisdom of yours?

COLE: There are no real choices in this world. Are there? Just circumstances created with good or bad information.

ROLAND: Huh.

DEE: (*aside*) Sounds like bullshit to me.

COLE: Excuse me? You wanna speak the fuck up? Or do I have to listen to you mumble?

DEE: Nothing. It's nothing.

COLE: You're damn right it's nothing, you fucking mongoloid. You got nothing to say now, do you?

DEE: No. Forget it. I'm sorry.

COLE: Don't tell me to fucking forget it. Asshole.

ROLAND: Wait, what were you saying about circumstances? That sounded smart. Let's talk about that again.

COLE: Fine.

ROLAND: What are the circumstances?

COLE: The contract, Iraq, this place, this fucking bullshit.

ROLAND: What fucking bullshit?

COLE: Being put here!

ROLAND: You put yourself here. You signed the contract. You did everything to put yourself in this position.

COLE: That's right, I did. But in that very same contract they used manipulative language to make it seem as if I had an out -- that we all had an out. They put me here and told me to bite my tongue and everything would be fine.

ROLAND: Wait a minute, there are no guarantees that things will be 'fine'. That's so fucking naive. Is that for real?

COLE: It's real. People, like those fucks at Trustwell: the Daria's of the world, the sadists who twist and turn everything in their favor. They want to trap us here, they want to stick us in this maze and make us dance on command. Fine! If that's the case, I will be the best dancer of the bunch. I will do what *I* feel needs to be done. Not you or not some fucking suit with a complex is going to tell me how to do my job. Is that clear?

ROLAND: (*pause*) Alright. Okay. Do you realize that there are at least two people behind that door-

COLE: Four. Four people behind that door.

ROLAND: Fine. Four people who you've just threatened to shoot, dead, and when they find out what you've done they probably won't be as understanding as we've been. When they find *that*, you're done. As in, you're going to jail.

DEE: Yeah.

ROLAND: Let me just break this down for you. What's going to happen. They will take you to the State Department H.Q. down the road and they will place you under arrest for murder. They won't give a shit about your little chess analogies or any other rationalization you can come up with.

COLE: No, they won't.

ROLAND: You're damn right they won't care.

COLE: No. I mean, they won't arrest me. Not for murder anyway. Maybe for threatening people...maybe.

ROLAND: Then you're fucking delusional. This is a waste of our time. You fucked yourself, my friend. I'm not going to let you drag me into your shit. Come on, Dee.

COLE: You know why they won't arrest me?

ROLAND: (*pause*) Okay, why? This should be good.

COLE: Master Sgt. Caldwell, 82nd Airborne, Fort Bragg -- know him? Company Sergeant for 'E' Company?

ROLAND: I wasn't a paratrooper. I was in S.F.

COLE: I know, but maybe you heard of him while you were at Bragg. He had a long nasty scar running from his cheek to the middle of his neck -- guys used to called him Scarface behind his back. Mean motherfucker.

ROLAND: It rings a bell.

COLE: Everybody hated Master Sergeant Caldwell, Scarface. Myself included. But I'll be damned if that mean mothefucker wasn't smart as a whip. He used to ask us -- and this always stuck with me -- 'how does a lion get to be the king of the jungle?' We didn't say shit because we were afraid of giving a wrong answer. Then he'd say, 'by being the baddest motherfucker in the bush. That's how.' We wanna win? We wanna make some kind of difference? We gotta be the baddest motherfuckers in this shit-hole. We got to take no quarter and expect none in return. And this--(*pointing to the head*) --is me being all I can be. You fuck with me, I'm gonna cut your fucking head off and show it to your fucking family.

DEE: (*pause*) Oh my god.

ROLAND: Holy shit. Is that what you did? Is that why you were gone this whole time?

Cole produces a bloodied wallet. He opens it and goes through it until he finds an ID card.

COLE: (*reading*) Taziq Mohammed. Original name, huh?

ROLAND: (*pause*) This is the whole 'quieting you mind' thing, huh?

COLE: Yep. Zen, man, zen like a pen. Ha! Baddest motherfucker in the jungle, baby! (*to the head*) Cole got your number, faggot! You fucked up you bitch-ass piece of dogshit! I got your motherfucking number! Ha!

ROLAND: (*rising*) That's it. Fuck it.

COLE: Where you going?

ROLAND: I'm leaving. Let's go, Dee.

DEE: Happily.

COLE: You can't leave.

ROLAND: The fuck we can't.

COLE: (*pointing his rifle at them*) Yeah, the fuck you can't.

ROLAND: (*pause*) This how it's gonna be?

COLE: Looks that way.

ROLAND: You're sick, Cole. I don't know what happened to you--

COLE: Nothing happened to me!

ROLAND: But you're...I don't know, man...like I said, you're broken.

COLE: Fuck you.

ROLAND: Is that right? 'Cause I'm not the one who's fucked here. You...you're off on fucking Mars, man. Is this about Kelly and the baby? Look, I heard, man, and it's not your fault.

COLE: Sit down. Shut up.

ROLAND: It's her fault. She fucked up. Like everyone fucks up at some point or another. She did you wrong. No one's doubting that. But this is not the way. This is not the way. Now, you put the gun down and let us leave and I swear, on my mother's grave, that me and Dee will do everything in our power to see that they don't lock you up for this. Because this is real. We'll say that you found the head--

COLE: Sit down and shut up or so help me I will put a bullet through that arrogant fucking head of yours. (*to Dee*) You too.

DEE: Cole, man, this isn't funny. We gotta go.

COLE: Do you see me laughing? Sit your asses down.

Roland and Dee sit.

COLE: Let me tell you how it's gonna go. You, both of you, ain't gonna say shit about any of this. And you're gonna tell those apes outside to back off.

ROLAND: When can we leave?

COLE: (*pause*) I don't know. But you're not going to fuck me. No one is going to fuck me. This company is going to heel to me.

ROLAND: People are going to have questions, Cole. Not just for us but for you too. How do you plan on dealing with that? You can't just stick a gun in their face and expect it to all go away.

COLE: I know. They'll believe me, I'm very persuasive.

ROLAND: Are you? I hope so, because if this is any indicator of how you're going to go about it, then you truly are fucked. They're going to take you back to the States and they're going to put a needle in your arm for this. Or failing that, they're going to lock you up and throw away the key. You're going to rot away in some prison for the rest of your life. Or are you too fucking dense to see that?

COLE: Oh, I know what the consequences are.

ROLAND: Do you? All it takes is one word from me or Dee and your whole world comes crashing down around you.

COLE: I don't like your tone.

ROLAND: Well, get used to it, man, because this is the life you lead. Cause and effect. There is a consequence to every action in this life.

COLE: Oh, really?! No shit. But there ain't going to be any consequences. I don't give a shit what you say. These people are smarter than you are.

ROLAND: Well, who's smarter than you?

COLE: (*pause*) You sound like you wanna say something. You sound like you wanna start blabbing about all this.

ROLAND: I say let the punishment fit the crime. How does that strike you?

COLE: Don't test me.

ROLAND: Oh, I'm not testing you. I'm just asking. Or are you struggling with that one too?

COLE: Fuck you.

ROLAND: (*pause*) Yeah, fuck me. But you know

what, Cole? I don't give a shit. Do your worst. But I'll tell you, you better kill me or else I'm gonna come back and tear your throat out.

COLE: What are you getting at?

ROLAND: I'm gonna walk out there and I'm gonna tell them whatever the fuck I wish and none of your threats mean a good goddamn to me. Because here's the deal: you are coward of the absolute worst stripe. You have nothing to offer anyone. And you know that. You sit around bitching and moaning about your situation more than anyone I know. You have no capacity to deal with anyone or anything. I have seen children with more grounding than you. And worst of all, worst of all, you're mean and cruel. And if you don't believe me…(*re: the head*) ask that poor bastard or…go ask you wife.

Cole charges Roland--

COLE: You motherfucker!

Cole places the barrel of his gun against Roland's head.

COLE: Don't say another fucking word or you're dead.

ROLAND: (*a long pause*) Fuck. You.

Cole moves to shoot Roland but Roland knocks his rifle away and in a flash pulls a knife from his vest and plunges it into Cole's heart. He drags the knife downward, ripping Cole open.

DEE: Shit!

Roland removes the knife from Cole's chest. Cole dies. A long beat.

DEE: Jesus. What are we going to do? Roland, man, what are we going to say?

ROLAND: We're going to tell the truth. That's all.

Blackout.

ABOUT THE AUTHOR

Johnny Alspaugh is a writer, actor, and director originally from San Diego, California. He has a BA in Theater Arts from San Diego State University. His other plays include: *Hits the Fan* and *The Tango*. He currently resides in Brooklyn, New York.

www.ingramcontent.com/pod-product-compliance
Lightning Source LLC
Chambersburg PA
CBHW061335040426
42444CB00011B/2928